Bespoke

10 knit & crochet designs for you and your bike

baa
ram
ewe

ISBN 978-0-9927730-0-7

www.baaramewe.co.uk

Garments

Woodrup .... page 7
Maillot Jaune .... page 15
Hercules .... page 27

Accessories

Courier .... page 35
Picycle .... page 39
Helmet Head ....page 47
Frame .... page 51
Wickerton .... page 55
Peachy .... page 59
Chop Chop .... page 63

Other Stuff

knitting abbreviations..... page 65
crochet abbreviations...... page 66
acknowledgements............. page 67

contents

When news that the Tour de France was going to be held in Yorkshire, England, just a stone's throw from both our stores, we immediately thought of making a book of designs inspired by the bike to be worn to celebrate the arrival of the Tour and beyond. From our own knitted version of the yellow jersey to a cute granny circle saddle cover, it was great coming up with ideas for the collection and being inspired by the ideas shared by our designers.

We wanted the patterns to be as flexible as possible, whether that's giving you a large range of sizes for garments, different options for accessories, or instructions on how to customise a pattern to make it fit your bike. We know it's not just humans that come in different shapes and sizes - bicycles do too!

Finally, while we hope you enjoy the patterns in this book and have fun showing them off on the open road, please don't forget to stay safe! Wear a cycle helmet when riding your bike and make sure any accessories you do add to your bike don't interfere with the smooth operation of your two-wheeled friend.

Jo and Verity
baa ram ewe, January 2014

garments

Woodrup
by Ann Kingstone

Ann says:

The Woodrup cardigan is a top-down seamless knit, with short rows to slightly scoop the front neck and a circular yoke with colourwork elements. The yarn used in Woodrup is spun in the town where I was born and lived most of my life, Huddersfield.

Woodrup plays homage to the Leeds based cycle company who, for nearly half a century, have been synonymous with expertly made bicycle framesets. Their shop on the Kirkstall Road continues the Woodrup tradition, including frame-building, repair, restoration, and re-spray.

Yarn:

Rowan Fine Tweed

384 Monsal Dale   **376 Bell Busk**   **381 Richmond**   **387 Beresford**

(A) - Monsal Dale: 12 (13, 14, 15, 16) x 25g balls
(B) - Bell Busk: 2 (2, 2, 3, 3) x 25g balls
(C) - Richmond: 2 (2, 2, 3, 3) x 25g balls
(D) - Beresford: 1 (1, 1, 2, 2) x 25g balls

Tension:

26sts x 36rows = 10cm/ 4 inches measured over blocked St st.

Materials:

3mm 60cm circular for yoke and body
3mm DPNs for sleeves or 3mm or 80cm circular for magic loop method
6 x stitch markers
9 x 15mm diameter buttons

Sizes:

To fit up to 81 (86.5, 89.5, 96, 100.5)cm/32 (34, 35.25, 37.75, 39.5) in full bust measurement with 4-5cm/1-2in of positive ease

Yoke

With A, cast on 84 (96, 96, 96, 96) sts.
Row 1 and all odd rows: K1, *p2, k2; rep from * to last 3 sts, p2, k1.
Row 2 and all even rows: P1, *k2, p2; rep from * to last 3 sts, k2, p1.
Rep last 2 rows 5 times more.

Body set-up row: K1, *m1b, k2; rep from * to last st, m1b, k1, pm, cast on 10 sts using backwards loop method for steek sts, pm for beg of rnd. 136 (154, 154, 154, 154) sts.

Join to work in the rnd then commence short rows in the first rnd as follows:

Short Row 1 (RS): K100 (113, 113, 113, 113), w&t.
Short Row 2 (WS): P73 (82, 82, 82, 82), w&t.
Short Row 3 (RS): Knit to wrapped st of prev row, knit together the wrap and the st it wraps, k5, w&t.
Short Row 4 (WS): Purl to wrapped st of prev row, purl together the wrap and the st it wraps, p5, w&t.

Rep last two Short Rows 2 (3, 3, 3, 3) times more.

Next rnd (RS): Knit to wrapped st of prev row, knit together the wrap and the st it wraps, knit to end of rnd.

Next rnd: Knit to the rem wrapped st, knit together the wrap and the st it wraps, knit to end of rnd.

Work 15 rnds in St st. Break A and join C.

Inc Rnd: K1, *m1b, k2; rep from * to 1 st before first marker, m1b, k1, then turn without slipping the marker. 199 (226, 226, 226, 226) sts

Work applied i-cord to beg of rnd marker. Break off C.

With RS facing and B, pu and knit 189 (216, 216, 216, 216) sts along the i-cord (1 st for every row of i-cord, picked up through edge of the i-cord sts that are immediately next to the WS purl sts). Slm, k10, slm.

Begin colourwork:

Colourwork Rnd: Work chart, working repeat 7 (8, 8, 8, 8) times across to next marker, slm, k10 with B, slm.

Cont in patt as set to end of Rnd 22 of chart. 283 (322, 322, 322, 322) sts

Break B and join C, then knit to first marker. Do not slm. Turn.

Work applied i-cord to beg of rnd marker. Break off C.

With RS facing and A, pu and knit 273 (312, 312, 312, 312) sts along the i-cord (1 st for every row of i-cord, picked up through edge of the i-cord sts that are immediately next to the WS purl sts). Slm, k10, slm.

Continuing in A, knit 8 (10, 9, 6, 7) rnds in St st, then place sleeve markers as follows:

Set-up Rnd: K39 (45, 45, 46, 46), pm, k54 (62, 62, 60, 60), pm, k87 (98, 98, 100, 100), pm, k54 (62, 62, 60, 60), pm, k39 (45, 45, 46, 46), slm, k10, slm.

Now inc as follows every alt rnd 3 (2, 3, 4, 4) times, then inc every rnd 3 (3, 3, 4, 5) times more.

Inc Rnd: [Knit to 1 st before marker, m1b, k1, slm, k1, m1f] four times, knit to marker, slm, k10, slm.

331 (362, 370, 386, 394) sts after all inc rnds have been completed.

Body

Dividing Rnd: [Knit to marker, remove m, place all sts to next marker on holder, cast on 6 (5, 6, 7, 9) sts, slm, cast on 6 (5, 6, 7, 9) sts] twice, knit to marker, slm, k10, slm. 223 (238, 246, 262, 274) sts

Work 18 rnds in St st.

Shape bust:

Dec Rnd: [Knit to 2 sts before marker, k2tog, slm, ssk] twice, knit to marker, slm, k10, slm. 4 sts dec'd

Rep Dec Rnd every following 5th rnd 9 times more. 183 (198, 206, 222, 234) sts

Work 20 rnds even in st st, or to desired length to beg of hip shaping.

Shape hips:

Inc Rnd: [Knit to 1 st before marker, m1b, k1, slm, k1, m1f] twice, knit to marker, slm, k10, slm. 4 sts inc'd

Rep Inc Rnd every 4th rnd 9 times more. 223 (238, 246, 262, 274) sts

Knit 2 rnds.

Next Rnd: Knit, removing side markers and decreasing 1(0, 0, 0, 0) st approx midway in rnd. 222 (238, 246, 262, 274) sts

Ribbed Hem:

Set-up Rnd: K1, *p2, k2; rep from * to 3 sts before first marker, p2, k1, rm, cast off next 10 sts, removing marker. 212 (228, 236, 252, 264) sts

Row 1 (RS): K1, *p2, k2; rep from * to last 3 sts, p2, k1. Turn.
Row 2 (WS): P1, *k2, p2; rep from * to last 3 sts, k2, p1. Turn.

Rep last 2 rows 11 times more. Cast off.

Sleeves (make 2)

Place the 66 (72, 74, 76, 78) held sts from one sleeve onto your needle(s).
Join A and knit across, then pu and knit 12 (10, 12, 14, 18) sts from underarm cast-on. Join to work in the rnd. 78 (82, 86, 90, 96) sts

Set up Rnd: K72 (77, 80, 83, 87), pm. From this point on all rnds begin and end at this marker.

Work 26 rnds in St st.

Dec Rnd: Ssk, knit to 2 sts before marker, k2tog, slm. 2 sts dec'd

Rep Dec Rnd every foll 12th (12th, 10th, 9th, 8th) rnd 6 (6, 8, 4, 11) times more, then every foll 11th (11th, 9th, 8th, 7th) rnd 4 (4, 4, 10, 4) times more. 56 (60, 60, 60, 64) sts

Next 16 Rnds: *K2, p2; rep from * to end.

Cast off.

Steek

Press the steek with a steam iron on the lowest setting that will provide steam. To protect the work, place a damp cloth between the iron and the work as you press.

Then cut along the centre of the steek, between the fifth and sixth st columns.

Apply reinforcement along the steek on each cardigan front; either by sewing a line of short machine sts along it, or crochet a line of slip-st crochet along it.

Buttonhole Band

With C and RS facing, pu sts from right front as follows:

Pick-up Row: Pu and knit 18 sts along ribbed hem (3 sts for every 4 rows of rib). Then, holding the yarn on the WS, pull loops through to the RS between the main fabric and the first st column in the steek. Working in this manner, make sts at the rate of 3 sts for every 4 rows. Then pu and knit 9 sts along the edge of the neck rib (3 sts for every 4 rows). Finally cast on 3 sts next to the last st you have made.

Turn the work and, still working with C, work applied i-cord to end of row.

Change to A and pu and knit sts along the full length of the applied i-cord, picking up 1 st for each row of i-cord and picking up from the edge of each i-cord st that is next to the steek, ie. on the WS.

Knit one row, evenly decreasing to the nearest multiple of 4 sts plus 2 sts.

Row 1: *K2, p2; rep from * to last 2 sts, k2.

Row 2: *P2, k2; rep from * to last 2 sts, p2.

Now mark the centre points for 9 evenly spaced buttonholes, placing the first and last markers approx 2cm from the top and bottom of the cardigan. To mark, either fasten a safety pin to the strand between two sts, or pull a short length of yarn through between sts on the needle. Then work 2 buttonhole rows as follows:

Buttonhole Row 1: *Work in 2x2 rib as established to 1 st before marker, then sl1 p-wise wyif, take yarn back, (sl1 p-wise wyif, psso) twice, sl1 back to LH needle, turn and cable cast on 3 sts, turn; rep from * until you have worked the last buttonhole, then work in 2x2 rib as established to end.

Buttonhole Row 2: *Work in 2x2 rib as established to 1 st before end of first cable cast on, sl1 p-wise, work next st in patt, psso; rep from * until the last buttonhole has been completed, then work in 2x2 rib as established to end.

Cont in rib as established for a further 3 rows, then cast off in 2x2 rib patt.

Buttonband

With C and RS facing, pick up same number of sts as for buttonhole band from neck of left front to hem. Cont as for Buttonhole band, omitting buttonhole rows and instead working a total of 7 rows in 2x2 rib.

Finishing

Weave in all ends. You may also wish to trim the steek edges and sew them to the WS using a herringbone hemstitch or whipstitch. Apply buttons. Block the cardigan to the dimensions shown in schematic.

Special instructions

m1b: from behind insert the LH needle into the background colour strand between the needles, then k the strand.
m1f: from the front insert LH needle into the background colour strand between the needles, then knit the strand tbl.

In colourwork rnds occasionally trap (weave in) the stranding yarn during runs of more than 9 sts in one colour. Take care to keep traps at least one st apart when trapping in consecutive rnds.

Applied I-cord (WS): Cast on 3 sts to LH needle, then *k2, ssk, return 3 sts to LH needle; rep from * to beg of rnd marker, cast off the 3 i-cord sts, turn so RS is facing for next row.

Please refer to the tutorials section at www.annkingstone.com to see demonstration videos for trapping floats, steeking, picking up sts next to a steek, working applied i-cord and picking up sts from applied i-cord.

Chart

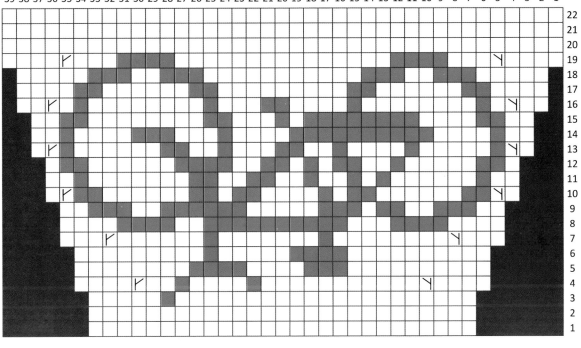

Key ⬛ No stitch ⬜ Knit in B 🟦 Knit in D ⅄ m1f in B Γ m1b in B

Schematic

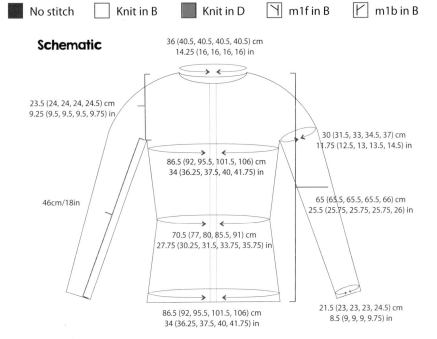

36 (40.5, 40.5, 40.5, 40.5) cm
14.25 (16, 16, 16, 16) in

23.5 (24, 24, 24, 24.5) cm
9.25 (9.5, 9.5, 9.5, 9.75) in

30 (31.5, 33, 34.5, 37) cm
11.75 (12.5, 13, 13.5, 14.5) in

86.5 (92, 95.5, 101.5, 106) cm
34 (36.25, 37.5, 40, 41.75) in

65 (65.5, 65.5, 65.5, 66) cm
25.5 (25.75, 25.75, 25.75, 26) in

46cm/18in

70.5 (77, 80, 85.5, 91) cm
27.75 (30.25, 31.5, 33.75, 35.75) in

86.5 (92, 95.5, 101.5, 106) cm
34 (36.25, 37.5, 40, 41.75) in

21.5 (23, 23, 23, 24.5) cm
8.5 (9, 9, 9, 9.75) in

page 13

Maillot Jaune

by Alison Moreton

Alison says:

The rib design in the yoke of Maillot Jaune is inspired by the radiating spokes of a bicycle wheel. This is echoed in the rib at cuffs and hem.

The sweater is worked from top down. The top of yoke is worked flat, and then button bands are picked up and knitted.

Yarn:

Rowan Pure Wool Worsted

132 Buttercup   **125 Olive**

Children's sizes require 2 (2, 2, 3, 3, 4, 4, 5, 5) balls
Women's sizes require 5 (5, 6, 6, 7, 7, 7, 8, 8, 9, 9, 9) balls
Men's sizes require 7 (8, 9, 10, 11) balls

Tension:

20sts x 28rows = 10cm/ 4 inches measured over stocking stitch.

Materials:

4.5mm circular needle (40cm length for babies' sizes, 60cm for children's sizes, 80/100cm for adults' sizes), 4.5mm dpns, 4mm straight or circular needles.
Scrap yarn
Stitch markers – 1 for children's and men's sizes, 2 for women's sizes.
Buttons: 10-14mm diameter
children's sizes require 4 (5, 5, 5, 6, 6, 6, 6, 7)
women's sizes require 7 (7, 7, 7, 7, 7, 7, 8, 8, 8, 8, 8)
all men's sizes require 8

Sizes:

Children's sizes to fit 6-9 months (12-18mo, 18-24mo, 2-3yrs, 4-5yrs, 6-7yrs, 8-9yrs, 10-11yrs, 12-13yrs), 51 (54, 56, 61, 67.5, 71, 76, 81.5, 86.5) cm/20 (21.25, 22, 24, 26.5, 28, 30, 32, 34) in finished chest

Women's sizes 81.5 (86.5, 91.5, 96.5, 101.5, 106.5, 112, 117, 122, 127, 132, 137) cm/32 (34, 36, 38, 40, 42, 44, 46, 48, 50, 52, 54) in finished bust; intended to fit with 0-5cm/0-2in of positive ease

Men's sizes S (M, L, XL, XXL), 96.5 (106.5, 117, 127, 137) cm/38 (42, 46, 50, 54) in finished chest, intended to fit with 5-10cm/2-4in of positive ease

Yoke

Using 4.5mm circular needle, cast on A __ sts. Do not join.

Row 1 (WS): P1, *k1, p1; rep from * to end.
Row 2 (RS): K1, *p1, k1; rep from * to end.

Rep last two rows once more.

Inc row: *P1, k1, p1, kfb; rep from * to last 3 sts, p1, k1, p1. (B sts)

Next row (RS): *K1, p1, k1, p2; rep from * to last 3 sts, k1, p1, k1.

Next row: *P1, k1, p1, k2; rep from * to last 3 sts, p1, k1, p1.

Rep last two rows C __ more times.

Next row (RS): *K1, p1, k1, p2; rep from * to last 3 sts, k1, p1, k1.

Inc row: *P1, kfb, p1, k2; rep from * to last 3 sts, p1, kfb, p1. (D __ sts)

Next row (RS): K1, *p2, k1; rep from * to end.

Next row: P1, *k2, p1; rep from * to end.

Rep last two rows E __ more times.

Begin short rows to raise back neck:

Next row (RS): K1, *p2, k1; rep from * to 24 sts before end of row, p2, k1, p1, w&t.

Next row: K1, p1, *k2, p1; rep from * to 21 sts before end of row, k1, w&t

Next row: Work in rib patt to 3 sts before wrapped st, w&t

Rep this row 3 times more.

Next row (RS): Work in rib patt to end. (End of short rows.)

Inc row (WS): *P1, k2, p1, kfb, k1; rep from * to last 4 sts, p1, k2, p1. (F __ sts)

Next row: *K1, p2, k1, p3; rep from * to last 4 sts, k1, p2, k1.

Next row: *P1, k2, p1, k3; rep from * to last 4 sts, p1, k2, p1.

Rep last two rows G __ more times.

Next row: *K1, p2, k1, p3; rep from * to last 4 sts, k1, p2, k1.

Inc row (WS): *P1, kfb, k1, p1, k3; rep from * to last 4 sts, p1, kfb, k1, p1. (H __ sts)

Next row: K1, *p3, k1; rep from * to end.

Next row: P1, *k3, p1; rep from * to end.

Rep last two rows J __ more times.

Next row (RS): K1, *p3, k1; rep from * to end.

Begin buttonbands:

Buttonbands are worked with a second ball of yarn. Leave original yarn attached to yoke; you will continue working with this later.

Girl's/Woman's Sizes Only:

Buttonhole band:

Using 4mm needles and second ball of yarn, and with RS facing, pick up and knit K __ sts up right edge of yoke (this is the end where the working yarn is), starting at end nearest to last st worked.

Row 1: *P1, k2tog, yo, k1; rep from * to last st, k1.

Row 2: P1, *p3, k1; rep from * to end.

Row 3: *P1, k3; rep from * to last st, k1.

Cast off in patt.

Buttonband:

Using 4mm needles and with RS facing, pick up and knit K __ sts down left edge of yoke, starting at cast on edge.

Row 1: K1, *k3, p1; rep from * to end.

Row 2: *K1, p3; rep from * to last st, p1.

Row 3: Work as Row 1.

Cast off in patt.

Boy's / Men's Sizes Only:

Buttonband:

Using 4mm needles and second ball of yarn, and with RS facing, pick up and knit K __ sts up right edge of yoke (this is the end where the working yarn is), starting at end nearest to last st worked.

Row 1: *P1, k3; rep from * to last st, k1.

Row 2: P1, *p3, k1; rep from * to end.

Row 3: Work as Row 1.

Cast off in patt.

Buttonhole band:

Using 4mm needles and with RS facing, pick up and knit K __ sts down left edge of yoke, starting at cast on edge.

Row 1: K1, *k3, p1; rep from * to end.

Row 2: *K1, p2tog, yo, p1; rep from * to last st, p1.

Row 3: Work as Row 1.

Cast off in patt.

All Sizes:

Return to yoke with main yarn and cont as foll with WS facing:

Next row (WS): *P1, k7; rep from * to last 5 sts, p1, k4. Pick up 3 sts each from bottom of each buttonband and place on separate DPNS. Overlap buttonbands with buttonband facing you on WS and buttonhole band behind it. With circular needle, *Knit tog 1 st from front DPN and 1 st from back DPN; rep from * twice more.

You are now working in the round inside out with WS facing you. PM for beg of rnd.

Next row (WS): *P1, k7; rep from * to end.

Rep last rnd L __ times more.

Knit M__ rnds even.

Separate sleeves and body:

Next rnd: Knit across N __ sts, place next P__ sts onto scrap yarn for sleeve, cast on Q__ sts for underarm, knit across R__ sts, place next P__ sts onto scrap yarn for sleeve, cast on Q__ sts for underarm, knit S__ sts. Remove marker. Knit across T__ sts, pm for new beg of rnd. (U__ body sts)

Body

Woman's Sizes Only:

Next rnd: K a__ , pm, knit to end of rnd.

Knit every rnd until work measures 5cm/ 2in from underarm cast on.

Dec rnd: [K3, k2tog, knit to 5 sts before marker, ssk, k3, slm] twice. 4 sts dec'd

Knit 6 rnds.

Rep last 7 rnds 3 more times. Work Dec rnd only once more. (b__ sts)

Knit 14 rnds.

Inc rnd: [K4, kfb, knit to 5 sts before marker, kfb, k4, slm] twice. 4 sts inc'd.

Knit 5 rnds.

Rep last 6 rnds 5 more times. Work Inc rnd only once more. (c__ sts)

Sizes 81.5, 101.5, 122: Next rnd: Knit.

Sizes 86.5, 106.5, 127: Next rnd: K4, kfb, k9, kfb, knit to 15 sts before marker, kfb, k9, kfb, k4, slm, k4, kfb, knit to 5 sts before marker, kfb, knit to end.

Sizes 91.5, 112, 132: Next rnd: [K4, kfb, knit to 5 sts before marker, kfb, k4, slm] twice.

Sizes 96.5, 117, 137: Next rnd: K4, kfb, knit to 5 sts before marker, kfb, knit to end.

(d__ sts)

Men's and Children's Sizes Only:

Next rnd: Knit. (a__ sts)

Rep this rnd until work measures b__ from underarm cast on.

Sizes 6-9mo, 4-5yrs, 6-7yrs: Next rnd: Knit, dec 4 sts evenly spaced around.

Sizes 12-18mo, 12-13yrs, Men's M, XL: Next rnd: Knit, dec 2 sts evenly spaced around.

Sizes 18-24mo, 8-9yrs, Men's S, L, XXL: Next rnd: Knit, inc 2 sts evenly spaced around

Sizes 2-3yrs, 10-11yrs: Next rnd: Knit.

(c__ sts)

All Sizes:

Hem:

Next rnd: *P1, k7; rep from * to end.

Rep this rnd 6 times more.

Next rnd: *P1, k3; rep from * to end.

Rep this rnd 6 times more.

Cast off in patt.

Sleeves

With WS facing and using dpns, place held sts for one sleeve onto needles. Pick up and knit e__ sts from underarm cast on. (f__ sts total). Knit g__ sts, pm for beg of rnd.

Knit h __ rnds.

Dec rnd: K1, k2tog, k to last 3 sts, ssk, k1. (j__ sts)

Knit k__ rnds.

Rep these l__ rnds until m__ sts remain.

Work Dec rnd once more. (n__ sts)

Knit p__ rnds.

Cuff

Next rnd: *P1, k7; rep from * to end.

Rep this rnd 5 times more.

Next rnd: *P1, k3; rep from * to end.

Rep this rnd 5 times more.

Cast off in patt.

Repeat for second sleeve.

Finishing

Weave in ends. Block, pinning cuffs, button bands and hem to lie flat. Sew on buttons.

Special Instructions

w&t: wrap and turn. Bring yarn to the front between the needles, slip the next st purlwise, take yarn to back between the needles, turn work, slip st back from LH to RH needle. Yarn is in front – if next st is knit, take yarn to back between the needles.

Hints and Tips

Construction notes: Sweater is worked from top down. Top of yoke is worked flat, then buttonbands are picked up and knitted. Stitches are picked up from bottom of buttonbands and yoke is joined in the round. Body and sleeves are knit in the round inside out so reverse stocking stitch will show on the RS after completion.

If you find holes form at the underarms after picking up sts for the sleeves, you can always pick up more sts – just decrease the extra sts in the next rnd.

The neck cast on is very stretchy – if it is not tight enough, you can use a crochet chain on the wrong side to stabilise it (tutorial at http://www.yarnharlot.ca/blog/archives/2008/02/24/hooking_because_i_have_to.html)

Tip: if you find it hard to see where the wrapped sts are when working short rows, place a marker between the wrapped st and the next st you work. Then you will work in patt to 3 sts before the marker.

Women's sizes

Yoke numbers:

Sizes(in)	32	34	36	38	40	42	44	46	48	50	52	54
A	119	127	135	143	151	159	167	175	183	191	199	207
B	148	158	168	178	188	198	208	218	228	238	248	258
C	2	3	3	3	3	3	3	4	4	4	4	4
D	178	190	202	214	226	238	250	262	274	286	298	310
E	3	3	3	3	3	3	3	4	4	4	4	4
F	207	221	235	249	263	277	291	305	319	333	347	361
G	3	3	3	3	3	3	3	4	4	4	4	4
H	237	253	269	285	301	317	333	349	365	381	397	413
J	3	3	3	3	3	3	3	4	4	4	4	4
K	29	29	29	29	29	29	29	33	33	33	33	33
L	3	4	6	8	8	8	8	8	8	8	8	8
M	0	0	0	0	2	3	5	2	4	6	8	10
N	32	35	37	40	43	45	48	50	53	55	57	59
P	52	54	58	61	63	66	69	72	75	78	83	86
Q	12	11	12	12	11	11	11	11	11	11	13	13
R	68	74	78	83	89	94	99	104	109	114	117	122
S	36	39	41	43	46	49	51	54	56	59	60	63
T	38	41	43	46	49	51	54	56	59	61	64	66
U	160	170	180	190	200	210	220	230	240	250	260	270

Body and sleeve numbers:

Sizes(in)	32	34	36	38	40	42	44	46	48	50	52	54
a	80	85	90	95	100	105	110	115	120	125	130	135
b	140	150	160	170	180	190	200	210	220	230	240	250
c	168	178	188	198	208	218	228	238	248	258	268	278
d	168	184	192	200	208	224	232	240	248	264	272	280
e	14	14	14	15	13	14	13	14	13	14	15	16
f	66	68	72	76	76	80	82	86	88	92	98	102
g	59	61	65	68	69	73	75	79	81	85	90	94
h	8	10	8	6	6	8	5	13	11	5	10	6
j	64	66	70	74	74	78	80	84	86	90	96	100
k	7	6	5	5	5	4	4	4	4	4	3	3
l	8	7	6	6	6	5	5	5	5	5	4	4
m	42	42	42	42	42	42	42	50	50	50	50	50
n	40	40	40	40	40	40	40	48	48	48	48	48
p	3	5	8	0	3	8	6	8	8	4	8	4

Men's sizes

Yoke numbers:

Sizes	S	M	L	XL	XXL
A	143	159	175	191	207
B	178	198	218	238	258
C	3	3	3	3	3
D	214	238	262	286	310
E	4	4	4	4	4
F	249	277	305	333	361
G	4	4	4	4	4
H	285	317	349	381	413
J	4	4	4	4	4
K	33	33	33	33	33
L	8	8	8	8	8
M	4	8	11	15	18
N	39	45	49	54	59
P	62	67	75	81	86
Q	13	12	14	14	13
R	82	93	101	111	122
S	43	48	52	57	63
T	46	51	56	61	66
U	190	210	230	250	270

Schematic

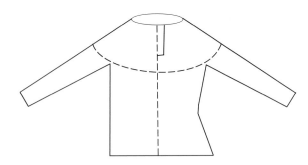

Note:

Left side depicts men's / children's sizes (no shaping)

Right side depicts women's sizes including waist shaping

Body and sleeve numbers:

Sizes	S	M	L	XL	XXL
a	190	210	230	250	270
b (cm)	35.5	38	38	38	38
b (in)	14	15	15	15	15
c	192	208	232	248	272
e	16	15	17	17	16
f	78	82	92	98	102
g	70	74	83	89	94
h	9	7	12	5	14
j	76	80	90	96	100
k	6	6	4	4	4
l	7	7	5	5	5
m	50	50	50	50	58
n	48	48	48	48	56
p	7	0	8	3	8

Children's sizes

Yoke numbers:

Sizes	6-9mo	12-18mo	18-24mo	2-3yrs	4-5yrs	6-7yrs	8-9yrs	10-11yrs	12-13yrs
A	71	75	79	87	95	103	111	119	127
B	88	93	98	108	118	128	138	148	158
C	0	1	1	1	1	2	2	2	2
D	106	112	118	130	142	154	166	178	190
E	1	1	1	1	2	2	2	2	3
F	123	130	137	151	165	179	193	207	221
G	1	1	1	1	2	2	2	2	3
H	141	149	157	173	189	205	221	237	253
J	1	1	2	2	2	2	2	3	3
K	17	21	21	21	25	25	25	25	29
L	2	4	4	4	4	4	4	4	4
M	0	0	0	0	0	0	2	2	2
N	19	21	21	24	27	29	32	34	37
P	30	31	34	37	38	42	45	48	51
Q	8	8	9	9	8	8	8	8	8
R	42	45	46	51	58	62	67	72	77
S	23	24	25	27	31	33	35	38	40
T	23	25	26	29	31	33	36	38	41
U	100	106	110	120	132	140	150	160	170

Body and sleeve numbers:

Sizes	6-9mo	12-18mo	18-24mo	2-3yrs	4-5yrs	6-7yrs	8-9yrs	10-11yrs	12-13yrs
a	100	106	110	120	132	140	150	160	170
b (cm)	11.5	13	14	16.5	20.5	23	24	25.5	28
b (in)	4.5	5	5.5	6.5	8	9	9.5	10	11
c	96	104	112	120	128	136	152	160	168
e	10	11	12	11	12	10	11	10	11
f	40	42	46	48	50	52	56	58	62
g	35	36	40	42	44	47	50	53	56
h	4	4	4	6	6	10	6	9	8
j	38	40	44	46	48	50	54	56	60
k	3	3	3	5	5	5	5	8	7
l	4	4	4	6	6	6	6	9	8
m	26	26	26	34	34	34	34	42	42
n	24	24	24	32	32	32	32	40	40
p	0	2	0	3	6	7	7	5	5

Women's sizes - finished measurements

Bust (in)	32	34	36	38	40	42	44	46	48	50	52	54
Bust (cm)	81.5	86.5	91.5	96.5	101.5	106.5	112	117	122	127	132	137
Yoke depth at front (in)	6.75	7.25	7.5	7.75	8.25	8.25	8.5	9.25	9.5	9.75	10.25	10.5
Yoke depth at front (cm)	17	18.5	19	19.5	21	21	21.5	23.5	24	25	26	26.5
Underarm to waist length (in)	7	7	7	7	7	7	7	7	7	7	7	7
Underarm to waist length (cm)	17.5	17.5	17.5	17.5	17.5	17.5	17.5	17.5	17.5	17.5	17.5	17.5
Waist to hem length (inches)	8.25	8.25	8.25	8.25	8.25	8.25	8.25	8.25	8.25	8.25	8.25	8.25
Waist to hem length (cm)	21	21	21	21	21	21	21	21	21	21	21	21
Hip (inches)	33.5	36.75	38.5	40	41.5	44.75	46.5	48	49.5	52.75	54.5	56
Hip (cm)	85	93.5	98	101.5	105.5	113.5	118	122	125.5	134	138.5	142
Upper arm circumference (in)	13.25	13.5	14.5	15.25	15.25	16	16.5	17.25	17.5	18.5	19.5	20.5
Upper arm circumference (cm)	33.5	34.5	37	38.5	38.5	40.5	42	44	44.5	47	49.5	52
Sleeve length underarm to cuff (in)	17.25	17.25	17.25	17.5	17.75	17.75	17.75	17.75	18.25	18.25	18.25	18.25
Sleeve length underarm to cuff (cm)	44	44	44	44.5	45	45	45	45	46.5	46.5	46.5	46.5

Children's sizes - finished measurements

Size	6-9mo	12-18mo	18-24mo	2-3yrs	4-5yrs	6-7yrs	8-9yrs	10-11yrs	12-13yrs
Chest / Hip (inches)	20	21.25	22	24	26.5	28	30	32	34
Chest / Hip (cm)	51	54	56	61	67.5	71	76	81.5	86.5
Yoke depth at front (inches)	4.5	5	5.25	5.25	5.75	6.25	6.5	6.75	7.25
Yoke depth at front (cm)	11.5	12.5	13.5	13.5	14.5	16	16.5	17	18.5
Underarm to hem length (inches)	6.75	7.25	7.75	8.75	10.25	11.25	11.5	12.25	13.25
Underarm to hem length (cm)	17	18.5	19.5	22	26	28.5	29	31	33.5
Upper arm circumference (inches)	8	8.5	9.25	9.5	10	10.5	11.25	11.5	12.5
Upper arm circumference (cm)	20.5	21.5	23.5	24	25.5	26.5	28.5	29	32
Sleeve length underarm to cuff (inches)	6.5	7.5	8.25	9.25	10.5	12.25	13.25	14.25	15.25
Sleeve length underarm to cuff (cm)	16.5	19	21	23.5	26.5	31	33.5	36	38.5

Men's sizes - finished measurements

Size	S	M	L	XL	XXL
Chest / Hip (inches)	38	42	46	50	54
Chest / Hip (cm)	96.5	106.5	117	127	137
Yoke depth at front (inches)	9.25	9.75	10.25	10.75	11.25
Yoke depth at front (cm)	23.5	25	26	27.5	28.5
Underarm to hem length (inches)	16	17	17	17	17
Underarm to hem length (cm)	40.5	43	43	43	43
Upper arm circumference (inches)	15.5	16.5	18.5	19.5	20.5
Upper arm circumference (cm)	39.5	42	47	49.5	52
Sleeve length underarm to cuff (inches)	18.25	19	19.75	20.25	20.75
Sleeve length underarm to cuff (cm)	46.5	48.5	50	51.5	52.5

Hercules

by Sarah Hatton

Sarah says:

This men's sweater was inspired by the tracks and patterns left by tyres in the mud which translated perfectly into simple elongated cables. The sweater is designed to be slouchy, with a 10cm/ 4 inch allowance.

Knitted in Handknit cotton, this gives the tyre track cables extra definition.

Yarn:

Rowan Handknit Cotton

347 Slate

18 (19, 20, 22, 23) x 50g balls

Tension:

20sts x 28rows = 10cm/ 4 inches measured over st st on larger needles
26sts x 28rows = 10cm/ 4 inches measured over chart patts on larger needles

Materials:

1 pair 3.25mm needles
1 pair 4mm needles
Cable needle
Tapestry needle
2 stitch holders

Sizes:

Finished chest circumference 108 (112, 118.5, 126.5, 130.5) cm/ 43.25 (45, 47.25, 50.5, 52.75) inches; designed to fit with approx. 5-10cm/2-4in positive ease

Back

Using 3.25mm needles, cast on 110 (116, 122, 128, 134) sts and purl 1 row.

Next row: K7, *m1, k3; rep from * 32 (34, 36, 38, 40) times more, m1, knit to end. 143 (151, 159, 167, 175) sts

Change to 4mm needles.

Row 1 (RS): P4 (0, 0, 4, 4), starting on st 17 (9, 5, 5, 1) of Chart A, work Chart A ending on st 24, work sts 1-16 of Chart B, work sts 1-24 of Chart A, work sts 1-16 of Chart B, work sts 1-7 of Chart C, work sts 1-16 of Chart B, work sts 1-24 of Chart A, work sts 1-16 of Chart B, work sts 1-8 (16, 20, 20, 24) of Chart A, p4 (0, 0, 4, 4).

Row 2: K4 (0, 0, 4, 4), work next 135 (151, 159, 159, 167) sts as set on row 2 of charts, k4 (0, 0, 4, 4).

These 2 rows set rev st st and chart placement.

Cont in patt as set until work meas 41 (42, 41, 42, 43) cm/16.25 (16.5, 16.25, 16.5, 17) in from cast on, ending after a WS row.

Shape armholes:

Cast off 5 sts at beg of next 2 rows. 133 (141, 149, 157, 165) sts

Next row (RS): P2, p2togtbl, patt to last 4 sts, p2tog, p2.

Next row: K3, patt to last 3 sts, k3.

Rep these 2 rows 4 times more. 123 (131, 139, 147, 155) sts

Next row (RS): P3, patt to last 3 sts, p3.

Next row: K3, patt to last 3 sts, k3. **

These 2 rows set rev st st at armhole edges. Working in chart patt where possible and all other sts in rev st st, cont as set until armhole meas 24 (25, 26, 27, 28) cm / 9.5 (9.75, 10.25, 10.75, 11) in, ending after a WS row.

Shape shoulders:

Cast off 13 (14, 15, 17, 18) sts at beg of next 2 rows. 97 (103, 109, 113, 119) sts

Cast off 14 (15, 16, 17, 18) sts at beg of next 4 rows. 41 (43, 45, 45, 47) sts

Leave sts on holder.

Front

Work as given for Back to **.

These 2 rows set rev st st at armhole edges. Working in patt where possible and all other sts in rev st st, cont as set until armhole meas 17 (18, 18, 19, 19) cm / 6.75 (7, 7, 7.5, 7.5) in, ending after a WS row.

Shape left front neck:

Next row (RS): Patt 52 (56, 60, 62, 66), turn and leave rem sts on a holder.

Dec 1 st at neck edge of next 8 rows, then on every foll alt row 3 (4, 5, 3, 4) times more. 41 (44, 47, 51, 54) sts

Cont without shaping until armhole matches Back to start of shoulder shaping, ending after a WS row.

Shape shoulders:

Cast off 13 (14, 15, 17, 18) sts at beg of next RS row, then 14 (15, 16, 17, 18) sts at beg of foll 2 RS rows.

Shape right front neck:

With RS of Front facing, leave centre 19 (19, 19, 23, 23) sts on holder for front neck, rejoin yarn to rem sts and patt to end.

Complete to match left front neck, reversing all shapings.

Sleeves (make 2)

Using 3.25mm needles, cast on 50 (54, 54, 56, 56) sts and purl 1 row.

Next row (WS): K1 (3, 3, 4, 4), [m1, k3] 14 (14, 14, 16, 16) times, m1, knit to end. 65 (69, 69, 73, 73) sts

Change to 4mm needles.

NB: When unable to work sts in patt, work sts in rev st st instead.

Row 1 (RS): Starting on st 12 (10, 10, 8, 8) of Chart A, work Chart A ending on st 24, work sts 1-16 of Chart B, work sts 1-7 of Chart C, work sts 1-16 of Chart B, work sts 1- 13 (15, 15, 17, 17) of Chart A.

Row 2: Work Row 2 of charts as set.

Cont in patt as set; AT THE SAME TIME, inc 1 st at each end of next row, then every 4th row 4 (2, 8, 10, 16) times more, then every foll 6th row 17 (19, 16, 15, 11) times more, working sts into patt when possible. 109 (113, 119, 125, 129) sts

Cont without shaping until sleeve meas 49 (52, 52, 53, 53) cm / 19.25 (20.5, 20.5, 20.75, 20.75) in from cast on, ending after a WS row.

Shape sleeve top:

Cast off 5 sts at beg of next 2 rows. 99 (103, 109, 115, 119) sts

Dec 1 st at each end of next row, then every alt row 4 times. 89 (93, 99, 105, 109) sts

Cast off 12 sts at beg of next 6 rows. 17 (21, 27, 33, 37) sts

Cast off rem sts.

Making Up

Join right shoulder seam.

Neckband

With RS facing and using 3.25mm needles, pick up and knit 25 (24, 27, 27, 28) sts down left side of neck, knit 19 (19, 19, 23, 23) sts from front neck holder, pick up and knit 25 (24, 27, 27, 28) sts up right side of neck, and knit 41 (43, 45, 45, 47) sts from holder at back neck. 110 (110, 118, 122, 126) sts

Row 1 (WS): K2, *p2, k2; rep from * to end.

Row 2: P2, *T2R, p2; rep from * to end.

Rep these 2 rows until neckband meas 6cm/ 2.25in from pick up, ending after a WS row.

Cast off in patt.

Join left shoulder and neckband seam. Join side and sleeve seams and set in sleeves. Weave in ends and block to measurements.

Special instructions

T2R – knit into front of 2nd st on LH needle, then knit into front of 1st st on LH needle and slip the two sts off needle together.

T2L – knit into back of 2nd st on LH needle, then knit first st on LH needle and slip the two sts off needle together.

1/1 LPC – Sl 1 to cn and hold in front, p1; k1 from cn.

1/1 RPC – Sl 1 to cn and hold in back, k1; p1 from cn.

1/2 RC – Sl 2 to cn and hold in back, k1; k2 from cn.

1/2 LC – Sl 1 to cn and hold in front, k2; k1 from cn.

Schematic

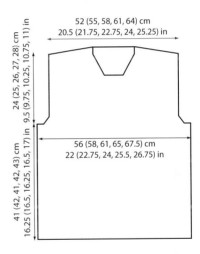

Chart A

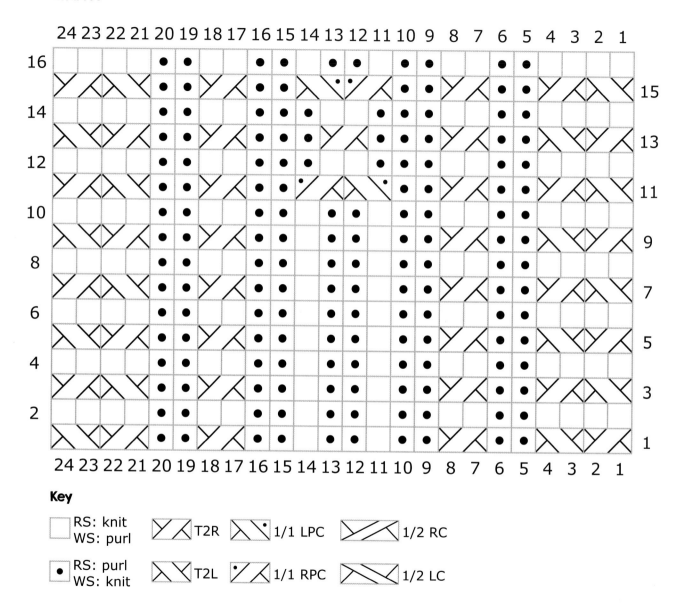

Key

RS: knit / WS: purl (empty box)	T2R	T2L
RS: purl / WS: knit (• dot)	1/1 LPC	1/1 RPC
	1/2 RC	1/2 LC

Chart B

Chart C

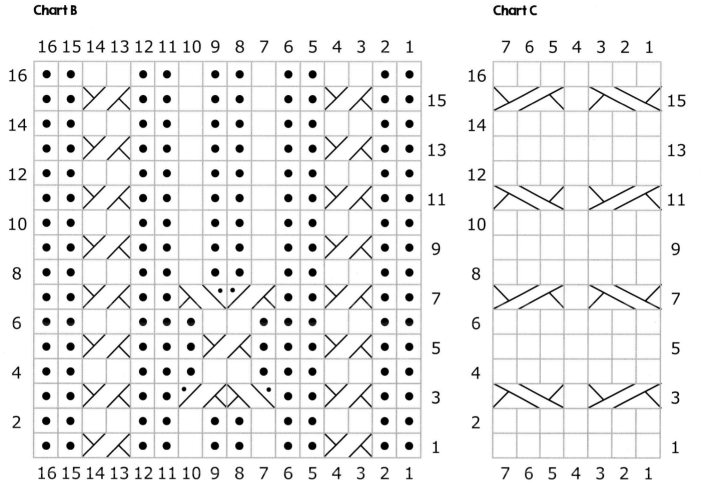

accessories

Courier

by Jo Spreckley

Jo says:

This messenger bag is a super simple knit in bold stripes. The bag is knitted and then felted in the washing machine to give it a great structure to hold all your belongings.

It's also a really easy project to customise, so put your own stamp on your bag as you pedal through the streets.

Sizes:

	Size before felting	Size after felting
Width	50cm/19.75in	42cm/16.5in
Height	45cm/17.75in	33cm/13in
Gusset	8cm/3.25in	6cm/2.5in
Flap	35cm/13.75in	25cm/10in
Strap	170cm/67in	130cm/51.25in

Yarn:

Rowan Big Wool

| 07 Smokey | 69 Resada | 68 Sun | 36 Glamour |

(A) - Smokey   3 x 100g ball
(B) - Resada   2 x 100g ball
(C) - Sun   1 x 100g ball
(D) - Glamour   1 x 100g ball

Tension:

Gauge is not vitally important, ours is 9 stitches and 12 rows to 10cm/ 4 inches

Materials:

10mm circular needle, 80cm long
Stitch markers
A stitch holder
2 magnetic bag poppers or buttons of your choice

Base

Using A, cast on 45 sts using the cable cast on method. Starting with a RS row, work in St st for 6 rows. Knit 3 rows, then work in St st for 7 rows more.

Fold work so the needle is parallel with the cast on edge and the RS is facing out; the fold line should be at the 3 knits rows.

Joining row (RS): *Knit 1 st from needle together with 1 st picked up from cast on edge; rep from * to end of row (45 sts on needle). Pick up and knit 5 sts from short edge of work, making sure to work through both layers of the base. Pick up and knit 45 sts along other edge of work, then pick up and knit 5 sts more from other short edge. Join to work in the rnd. Pm for beg of rnd. 100 sts

Body

Rnd 1 (ridge rnd): P1, pm, p44, pm, p6, pm, p44, pm, p5.

Rnd 2: P1, slm, k43, p1, slm, k5, p1, slm, k43, p1, slm, k5.

Rep Rnd 2, changing colours as follows:

4 rnds in A. 3 rnds in B. 2 rnds in A. 3 rnds in C. 2 rnds in A. 3 rnds in D. 10 rnds in A. 5 rnds in C. 2 rnds in A. 5 rnds in D. 2 rnds in A. 5 rnds in B. 3 rnds in A. 1 rnd in D. 2 rnds in A. 1 rnd in C. 2 rnds in A. 1 rnd in B. 4 rnds in A.

Alternatively, if working in a solid colour, rep last rnd 60 times more without colour changes.

Next rnd: With A, k51, cast off 43 sts, knit to end of row, remove marker, k1. Place last 7 sts just worked on holder for strap. 50 sts

Next row (RS): Sl1 p-wise, knit to last 7 sts before cast off, place last 7 sts of row on holder for strap. Turn. 43 sts

Flap

Row 1 (WS): Sl1 p-wise, purl to end.

Row 2 (RS): Sl1 k-wise, knit to end.

Rep these 2 rows, changing colours as follows:

8 more rows in A, 8 rows in B, 2 rows in A, 2 rows in C, 2 rows in A, 2 rows in D, 2 rows in A, 2 rows in C, 2 rows in A, 2 rows in B, 2 rows in A.

Alternatively, rep last 2 rows worked 17 times more, ending after a RS row (for 34 rows total).

Next row (WS): Sl1 p-wise, p2tog, purl to last 3 sts, p2tog, p1.

Cast off.

Strap

Transfer one set of 7 held sts to needle with RS facing. Join A.

Row 1 (RS): Knit.

Row 2 (WS): K1, p5, k1.

Repeat these 2 rows until strap measures 170cm/ 67in long from pick up.

Making sure the strap is not twisted, join the strap to the other set of 7 held sts using three-needle cast off.

Pockets (optional)

Cast on 20 sts and worked 10 rows in st st. Cast off.

Sew into bag, making sure to catch sts on inside of bag when sewing instead of going all the way through fabric of bag.

Finishing

Weave in ends on the inside of bag.

Felting

You need sufficient heat and agitation to make the bag felt. We washed it in one 40 degree C wash with a couple of old towels. If you need the bag to be denser and smaller, wash again. Once the bag is the right size for you, stuff it with an old towel or plastic bags and allow it to dry. You may want to iron your bag on the inside before it dries fully. This helps the strap dry flat as it may have a tendency to curl.

Apply fasteners between flap and bag. Alternatively, sew on button and crochet a chain loop, then sew in place to centre bottom edge of flap.

Now – on your bike!

Special instructions

Three-needle cast off: With WS facing, hold each needle parallel to each other and with third needle, knit 1 st from front needle and 1 st from back needle together, *knit 1 st from front needle and 1 st from back needle together, pass first stitch over second st on RH needle; rep from * to end, cut yarn and draw through rem st.

Hints & tips

Felting is not an exact science. You create a big bag, put it in the washing machine and it comes out smaller and denser. The amount of shrinkage in my test knits varied from 25% to 40%. My knitting shrank more in the rows than in the stitches. You may find yours is a little different. So, don't plan on your bag being precisely one size. Embrace the felty surprise!

I used 4 colours of Big Wool – I love a stripe. I settled on the mix of colours by knitting up a stripy test square and felting it. The finished bag weighs around 600g, so you could use 6 balls. My colour mix meant I needed 7 balls.

When folding the base, you may want to pin it in place before working the stitches together.

When changing colour, you can keep the yarn attached if you are going to reuse the shade within 3 rows. In this case, take the yarn loosely up the inside of the bag. If you are changing colour, leave a 10cm tail when starting or ending a colour. These ends should hang down on the inside of the bag as useful reminders of where your row starts and ends. You can weave these in at the end.

Schematic

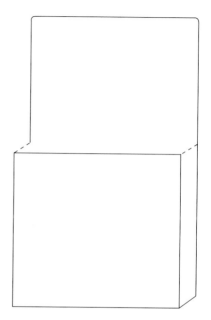

Karie says:

I love to navigate the streets of Glasgow on my beloved red bike, but I do miss biking in my native Denmark. Fewer hills!

The Picycle shawl was inspired by bicycles and their wheels. Like the Tour itself, the shawl is simple in construction, contains some sprint distances and may possess some tricky heights for the knitter to scale.

Yarn:

Rowan Kidsilk Haze

597 Jelly **666 Alhambra**

Full Circle (597 Jelly)   8 x 25g ball
Half Circle (666 Alhambra)   4 x 25g ball

Tension:

16sts x 20rows = 10cm/ 4 inches measured over blocked stocking stitch

Sizes:

Half Circle: 200cm/79in across; 100cm/39.5in depth
Full Circle: 200cm/79in diameter

Materials:

4.5mm circular needle 80cm long

4.5mm DPNs

Extra set of 4.5mm needles (optional)

4.5mm crochet hook

Stitch marker

Waste yarn for provisional cast-on – cotton in contrast colour

Tapestry needle (for grafting)

Full Circle Version

Cast on 9 sts. Divide evenly across 3 DPNs, join in the rnd being careful not to twist, pm to mark beg of rnd, and knit 1 rnd.

Rnd 2: *Yo, k1; rep from * to end of rnd. 18 sts

Knit 3 rnds.

Rnd 6: *Yo, k1; rep from * to end. 36 sts

Rnd 7: *K2tog, yo, k2; rep from * to end.

Rnd 8: Knit to end.

Rep Rnds 7-8 twice more.

Rnd 13: *Yo, k1; rep from * to end. 72 sts

Rnd 14: *K2tog, yo, k2; rep from * to end.

Rnd 15: Knit to end.

Repeat Rows 14-15 five times more.

Rnd 26: *Yo, k1; rep from * to end. 144 sts

Change to circular needles.

Rnds 27-28: Knit.

Work Rnds 1-21 of the Wheel Chart over all sts, working 16-st repeat 9 times in total across each rnd.

Rnd 50: Knit.

Rnd 51: *Yo, k1; rep from * to end. 288 sts

Rnd 52: *K2tog, yo, k2; rep from * to end.

Rnd 53: Knit to end.

Rep last two rnds 23 times more.

Rnd 100: *Yo, k1; rep from * to end. 576 sts

Rnds 101-103: Knit.

Work Rnds 1-21 of the Wheel Chart over all sts, working 16-st repeat 36 times in total across each rnd.

Rnds 125-129: Knit to end

Work Rnds 1-32 of Alps Chart twice, working 32-st repeat 18 times in total across each rnd.

Rnds 194-196: Knit to end.

Break yarn and leave sts on needle.

Edging

Using cotton waste yarn and crochet hook, provisionally cast on 19 sts onto DPNs or spare 4.5mm needles and knit 1 row. Change to working yarn.

Work Rows 1-12 of Edging Chart a total of 96 times, working last st of each WS row together with 1 st from RS of shawl body. Break yarn, leaving a long tail. Undo provisional cast on and place sts on other needle, then graft each end of edging together.

Weave in ends and block shawl to measurements, pinning out points.

Schematic

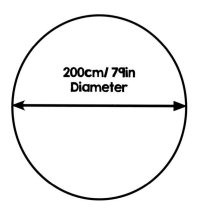

200cm/ 79in Diameter

Half Circle Version

Shawl Body

With circular needle, cast on 9 sts and knit 1 row.

Row 1 (RS): K3, *yo, k1; rep from * to last 2 sts, k2. 13 sts

Row 2 and all WS rows: K2, purl to last 2 sts, k2.

Row 3: Knit.

Row 5: K2, *yo, k1; rep to last 2 sts, k2. 22 sts

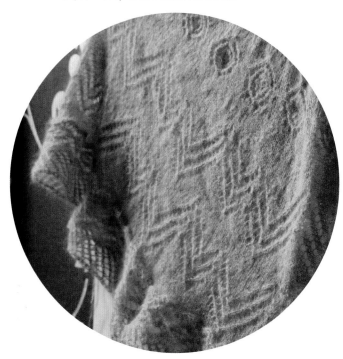

Row 6 (WS): K2, purl to last 2 sts, k2.

Row 7: K3, *k2tog, yo, k2; rep from * to last 2 sts, k3.

Rep last 2 rows twice more, then rep Row 6 once more.

Row 13: K2, *yo, k1; rep to last 2 sts, k2. 40 sts

Row 14 (WS): K2, purl to last 2 sts, k2.

Row 15: K2, *k2tog, yo, k2; rep from * to last 2 sts, k2.

Rep Rows 14-15 four times more, then rep Row 14 once more.

Row 25: K2, *yo, k1; rep from * to last 2 sts, k2. 76 sts

Row 27: K6, work Wheel Chart to last 6 sts, working 16-st repeat a total of four times, k6.

Cont in patt as set through Row 21 of Wheel Chart, then work 1 WS row.

Row 49: Knit

Row 51: K2, *yo, k1; rep from * to last 2 sts, k2. 148 sts

Row 52 (WS): K2, purl to last 2 sts, k2.

Row 53: K2, *k2tog, yo, k2; rep from * to last 2 sts, k2.

Rep last two rnds 22 times more, then work 1 WS row.

Row 99: K2, *yo, k1; rep from * to last 2 sts, k2. 292 sts

Row 101: Knit.

Row 103: K2, work Wheel Chart to last 2 sts, working 16-st repeat 18 times in total across row, k2.

Cont in patt as set through Row 21 of Wheel Chart. Work 1 WS row.

Rows 125 & 127: Knit.

Row 129: K2, work Alps Chart to last 2 sts, working 32-st repeat 9 times in total across row, k2.

Cont in patt as set through Row 32 of Alps Chart, then work Rows 1-32 of Alps Chart once more.

Rows 193 & 195: Knit.

Work 1 WS row.

Break yarn and leave sts on needle.

Edging

With spare 4.5mm needles, cast on 19 sts.

Row 1 (RS): Knit.

Row 2 (WS): Knit to last st, knit together last st of edging with 1 st from shawl body.

Rep last 2 rows once more.

Work Rows 1-12 of Edging Chart 48 times, working last st of each WS row together with 1 st from RS of shawl body.

Row 1 (RS): Knit.

Row 2 (WS): Knit to last st, knit together last st of edging with 1 st from shawl body.

Rep last 2 rows once more.

Cast off.

Weave in ends and block shawl to measurements, pinning out points.

Special instructions

5-st decrease: K2togtbl, k3tog, pass 2nd st on RH needle over 1st st on needle. 4 sts dec'd

Kfbf: Knit into front, back, and front of st. 2 sts inc'd

Wrap 3: Sl 3 wyif, yb, sl 3 sts back to LH needle and k3.

Only RS rows are charted for the Edging. All WS rows should be worked as purl to last st, purl together last st of edging and 1 st from RS of shawl body.

Hints & tips

If using stitch markers to separate repeats on Alps Chart, note that the markers should be placed after the Sl 1, k2tog, psso on Rows 13, 19 & 25

Schematic

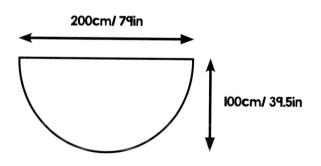

200cm/ 79in

100cm/ 39.5in

Alps Chart

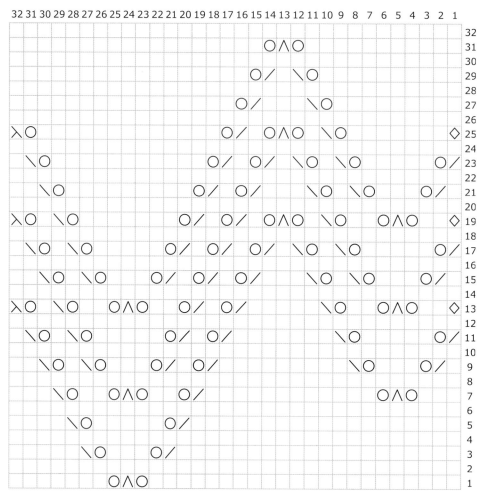

Edging Chart

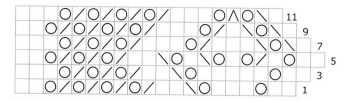

Wheel Chart

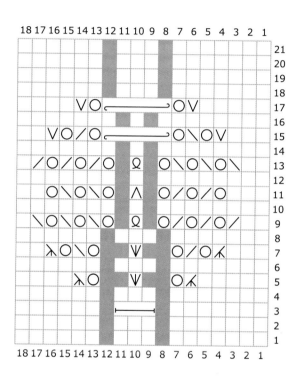

Key

☐ RS: knit; WS: purl	∧ Sl1, k2tog, psso	◇ Circular Shawl: 1st st of round only: Sl1, yo All other reps: yo
Q k tbl	⊢———⊣ RS: Wrap 3	Half Shawl: 1st st of row only: K1 All other reps: yo
O yo	⊂————⊃ 5-st decrease	▨ no stitch
V Kfb		
Ⅴ Kfbf	⊠ Circular Shawl: Last st of rnd only: Sl1, k2tog (removing beg of rnd marker) psso, replace marker All other reps: Sl1, k2tog, psso	
╱ K2tog		
╲ K2tog tbl	Half Shawl: Last st of row only: Ssk All other reps: Sl1, k2tog, psso	
⋏ K3tog		
⋋ K3tog tbl		

Helmet Head

by Sarah Alderson

Sarah says:

Being a doctor, I like to look cool and be safe so I never travel by bike without my groovy bike helmet. Sadly this does nothing for my coiffure once I reach my destination, and I look far less groovy once the helmet is off and the bike hair is on show.

This quick and easy colourful beanie is great for covering up those bike hair disasters and keeps me looking cool for the rest of the day.

Yarn:

Rowan Tweed

598 Monsal Dale   **599 Dove Dale**   **601 Beresford**

(A) - Monsal Dale
(B) - Beresford
(C) - Dove Dale

1 ball of each colour for all sizes

Tension:

17sts x 13rows = 10cm/ 4 inches measured over alternate rounds of htr and tr

Materials:

4mm Crochet Hook

Cable needle

2 stitch markers

Sizes:

S (M, L, XL)
To fit: Toddler (Child/Teen, Woman, Man) with 7.5cm (3inch) negative ease.
38 (43, 48, 53)cm / 15 (17, 19, 21) inch circumference
21 (24, 26, 29)cm / 7½ (9½, 10½, 11½) inch depth

Crown

Using A, 4ch.

Rnd 1: Work 5 (6, 7, 8)tr in first ch, ss to close rnd. (6 (7, 8, 9) sts)

Rnd 2: Join B, 2ch (counts as first htr throughout), htr in same st, *2htr in next st; rep from * to end, ss to close rnd. (12 (14, 16, 18) sts)

Rnd 3: Join C, 3ch (counts as first tr throughout), 2tr in next st, *work 1tr, 2tr in next st; rep from * to end, ss to close rnd. (18 (21, 24, 27) sts)

Rnd 4: With A, 2ch, htr in next st, 2htr in next st, *work 2htr, 2htr in next st; rep from * to end, ss to close rnd. (24 (28, 32, 36) sts)

Rnd 5: With B, 3ch, work 2tr, 2tr in next st, *work 3tr, 2tr in next st; rep from * to end, ss to close rnd. (30 (35, 40, 45) sts)

Rnd 6: With C, 2ch, work 3htr, 2htr in next st, *work 4htr, 2htr in next st; rep from * to end, ss to close rnd. (36 (42, 48, 54) sts)

Rnd 7: With A, 3ch, work 4tr, 2tr in next st, *work 5tr, 2tr in next st; rep from * to end, ss to close rnd. (42 (49, 56, 63) sts)

Rnd 8: With B, 2ch, work 5htr, 2htr in next st, *work 6htr, 2htr in next st; rep from * to end, ss to close rnd. (48 (56, 64, 72) sts)

Rnd 9: With C, 3ch, work 6tr, 2tr in next st, *work 7tr, 2tr in next st; rep from * to end, ss to close rnd. (54 (63, 72, 81) sts)

Rnd 10: With A, 2ch, work 7htr, 2htr in next st, *work 8htr, 2htr in next st; rep from * to end, ss to close rnd. (60 (70, 80, 90) sts)

Brim

Rnd 11: With B, 3ch, tr in each st to end, ss to close rnd.

Rnd 12: With C, 2ch, htr in each st to end, ss to close rnd.

Rnd 13: With A, 3ch, tr in each st to end, ss to close rnd.

Rnd 14: With B, 2ch, htr in each st to end, ss to close rnd.

Rnd 15: With C, 3ch, tr in each st to end, ss to close rnd.

Rnd 16: With A, 2ch, htr in each st to end, ss to close rnd.

Rep Rnds 11 - 16 a further 1 (2, 2, 3) times.

Sizes S & L only:

Rep Rnds 11 - 13 once more.

Next Rnd: With B, 1ch, dc in each st to end, ss to close rnd. Break yarn and weave in ends.

Sizes M & XL only:

Next Rnd: With C, 1ch, dc in each st to end, ss to close rnd. Break yarn and weave in ends.

Hints & tips

Do not break yarn between rounds; carry yarn up to next stripe. This hat is very stretchy so a larger amount of negative ease is needed.

Schematic

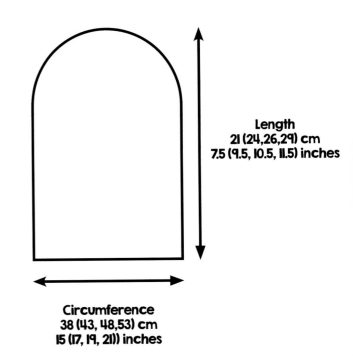

**Length
21 (24, 26, 29) cm
7.5 (9.5, 10.5, 11.5) inches**

**Circumference
38 (43, 48, 53) cm
15 (17, 19, 21)) inches**

Frame Mitts
by Rachel Coopey

Rachel says:

Inspired by the geometric shapes of bicycle frames, the cable motif on these mitts are mirrored across the pair.

Choose from two different lengths to knit- a short, wrist length version perfect for popping in your pockets, or longer arm-length ones for those super windy days.

Sizes:

Hand Circumference: 18.5 (20.5) cm/ 7.25 (8) in, designed to fit with up to 2cm/ 1in negative ease

Length: Short: 15.5cm/6in, Long: 31cm/12.25in

Yarn:

Rowan Fine Tweed

384 Monsal Dale   **385 Dove Dale**

Short - 2 balls
Long - 3 balls

Tension:

32sts x 50rows = 10cm/ 4in measured over stocking stitch

Materials:

2.5mm circular needle 80cm long or DPNs

Cable needle
5 stitch markers
stitch holder or waste yarn

Short Version

Cast on 58 (66) sts and join to work in the round, being careful not to twist sts. PM for beg of rnd.

**NB: When working charts, beg with Rnd 1 for Right Mitt and Rnd 9 for Left Mitt.

Next rnd: P2, k2, work 24 sts of chart, k2, [p2, k2] to end.
Rep this rnd 15 more times, ending on Rnd 16 of chart for Right Mitt and Rnd 8 for Left Mitt.

Next rnd: K4, work chart, knit to end.
Rep this rnd 5 more times.

Begin Thumb Gusset:

Left Mitt Only: K4, work chart, knit to last 2 (6) sts, pm, yo, pm, knit to end.
Right Mitt Only: K4, work chart, k6 (10), pm, yo, pm, knit to end.

Both Mitts:

Rnd 1: K4, work chart, knit to marker, slm, m1, k1tbl, m1, slm, knit to end.
Rnd 2: K4, work chart, knit to end.
Rnd 3: K4, work chart, knit to marker, slm, m1, knit to marker, m1, slm, knit to end.
Rep Rnds 2-3 nine times more. 23 sts between markers; 81 (89) sts total

Next rnd: K4, work chart, knit to marker, remove marker, place next 23 sts on a piece of waste yarn, remove marker, knit to end of rnd.

Work even in pattern as set until 16 rows of chart have been completed a total of 4 times for short version or 9 times for long version from cast on edge, ending on Rnd 16 of Chart for Right Mitt and Rnd 8 of Chart for Left Mitt.

Next rnd: P2, k2, work chart, k2, [p2, k2] to end.
Rep this rnd 10 times more. Cast off loosely in pattern.

Thumb:

Knit across 23 sts held for thumb, pick up and knit 2 sts from gap, and join to work in the rnd. PM for beg of rnd. 25 sts
Dec rnd: K23, k2tog. 24 sts

Knit 5 rnds.
Rib rnd: *K2, p2; rep from to end.
Rep this rnd 3 more times, then cast off loosely in pattern.

Weave in ends and block gently.

Long Version

Cast on 86 (94) sts and join to work in the round, being careful not to twist sts. PM for beg of rnd.
NB: When working charts, beg with Rnd 1 for Right Mitt and Rnd 9 for Left Mitt.

Next rnd: P2, k2, work 24 sts of chart, k2, p2, pm, k16, pm, [p2, k2] 5 (7) times, p2, pm, k16.
Rep this rnd 6 more times, slipping markers instead of placing them, and ending on Rnd 7 for Right Mitt and Rnd 15 for Left Mitt.

Dec rnd: P2, k2, work chart, k2, p2, slm, ssk, knit to 2 sts before marker, k2tog, slm, [p2, k2] 5 (7) times, p2, slm, ssk, knit to 2 sts before end, k2tog. 4 sts dec'd
Work 7 rnds even in patt.
Rep last 8 rnds twice more. 74 (82) sts

Rep Dec rnd.
Work 15 rnds even in patt.
Rep last 16 rnds twice more, then rep Dec rnd once more, removing all markers except beg of rnd marker on last rnd and ending on Rnd 16 of chart for Right Mitt and Rnd 8 of Chart for Left Mitt. 58 (66) sts

Work as for Short Version from ** to end.

Special Abbreviations

C4B: Slip next 2 sts to cn and place at back of work, k2; then k2 from cn.

C4F: Slip next 2 sts to cn and place at front of work, k2, then k2 from cn.

C3B: Slip next st to cn and place at back of work, k2, then p1 from cn.

C3F: Slip next 2 sts to cn and place at front of work, p1, then k2 from cn.

Chart

Columns: 24 23 22 21 20 19 18 17 16 15 14 13 12 11 10 9 8 7 6 5 4 3 2 1

Rows (right side): 16 15 14 13 12 11 10 9 8 7 6 5 4 3 2 1

Key

☐ knit	⟋⟍ C4F	⟋• C3F	
● purl	⟍⟋ C4B	•⟍ C3B	

Schematic

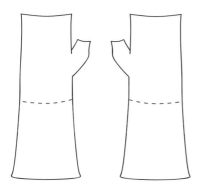

Wickerton
by Julie Glaze

Julie says:

The simple organic shaping of this bike basket uses just double crochet which means it looks impressive but is still suitable for beginners.

As I have an engineering background, my first thoughts about this design were how to attach it to the bike securely and keep its shape as a basket, the answer came after a bit of experimenting with a coat hanger ultimately solving both problems at once!

Yarn:

Rowan All Seasons Chunky

615 Whirlpool   **608 Heatwave**   **600 Foam**   **611 Samphire**

(A) - Whirlpool (615) x 2 balls
(B) - Heatwave (608) x 1 ball
(C) - Foam (600) x 1 ball
(D) - Samphire (611) x 1 ball

Tension:

13 sts x 15 rows = 10cm /4inches in double crochet

Materials:

5mm hook (UK 6/US 8/H)
Stitch markers/safety pins x 7
Wire coat hanger

Sizes:

Finished basket: width 33cm, depth 25cm (excluding coat-hanger hook), height 19cm

Base

Using A, work 21ch.
Row 1 (RS): Sk first ch, 20dc, turn. (21 sts)
Row 2 (WS): 1ch (counts as first dc throughout), 2dc into first st, 19dc, turn. (22 sts)
Rows 3-12: 1ch, 2dc into first st, dc to end, turn. (Row 12 = 32 sts)
Row 13: 1ch, dc to end, turn.
Row 14: 1ch, dc2tog, 26dc, dc2tog, dc into tc, turn. (30 sts)
Rows 15-19: 1ch, dc2tog, dc to third st from end, dc2tog, dc into tc, turn. (Row 19 = 20 sts)
Row 20: 1ch, dc around the outside of the base (6 sides) including 1dc in each row end and 2dc in each corner, fasten off.

Sides

Rnd 1: With the inside of the piece facing, join B at centre back (centre of Row 1) and work 1ch, dc in flo to end, ss to tc, fasten off, turn. (94 sts)

Place a stitch marker to mark position of each of the 6 corners plus 1 at centre front (7 total, see diagram). Move stitch markers up every few rows.

Rnd 2: Join C above ss, work 1ch, dc to end working 2dc above each st marker, ss to tc, fasten off, turn. (101 sts)

Remove stitch markers 1 and 7 (ie. back edge), leaving remaining stitch markers in place.

Rnd 3: Join D above ss, work 1ch, dc to end, ss into tc fasten off, turn.
Rnd 4: Join A above ss, work 1ch, dc to end, ss into tc fasten off, turn.
Rnd 5: Join B above ss, work 1ch, dc to end working 2dc above each stitch marker, ss to tc, fasten off, turn. (105 sts)
Rnds 6–11: Rep Rnds 3-5, changing colours as set. (Rnd 11 = 116 sts)
Remove stitch markers 3, 4 and 5, leaving remaining stitch markers in place (ie the widest points at sides).

Rnd 12: Join colour A above ss, 1ch, dc to end, ss into tc, fasten off, turn.
Rnd 13: Join colour B above ss, 1ch, dc to end, ss into tc, fasten off, turn.
Rnd 14: Join colour C above ss, 1ch, dc to end working 2dc above each stitch marker, ss into tc, fasten off, turn. (118 sts)

Rnds 15–17: Rep Rnds 12-14, changing colour as set. (Rnd 17 = 120 sts)
Remove remaining stitch markers.

Rnds 18-27: Changing colours as set work 1ch, dc to end, ss into tc, turn.
Rnd 28: Join A above ss, 1ch, dc to end, ss into tc, turn.
Rnd 29: Ss into dc twice, 1ch, dc to third st from end working over coat hanger wire, (do not join, this provides a gap for the coat-hanger hook) turn.

Cuff

Rnds 30-35: Using A, work 1ch, dc to end, turn and fasten off after Rnd 35.

Yorkshire Rose Motif

Using B, ch3.
Rnd 1: 9htr into 3rd ch from hook, ss into 3rd ch, fasten off.

Rnd 2: Join C with ss to front loop of any htr, work *2ch, [1htr, 1tr, 1htr] into flo of next htr, 2ch, ss into flo of next htr; rep from * a further 4 times finishing with ss into flo 1st st, turn.

Rnd 3: With WS facing, working behind Rnd 2 petals, ss into blo of next htr on Rnd 1 (centre of petal), *ch3, sk next htr, ss into blo of next htr on Rnd 1; rep from * a further 4 times finishing with ss into blo of 1st st, turn.

Rnd 4: With RS facing, working behind Rnd 2 petals, *ss into next 2ch sp, 3ch, [1tr, 2dtr, 1tr] into same 3ch sp, 3ch; rep from * a further 4 times, ss into first st, fasten off, turn.

Rnd 5: With WS facing, join D with ss to centre of any petal, working behind Rnd 4 petals, work *4ch, ss to centre of WS of next petal; rep from * a further 4 times, turn.

Rnd 6: With RS facing, working behind Rnd 4 petals, *ss into next 4ch sp, 3ch, [1tr, 2ch, ss into second ch from hook (picot formed), 1tr, 3ch, ss] into same 4ch sp; rep from * a further 4 times, fasten off.

Finishing

Weave in ends.

Sew the Rose to the front cuff of the basket.

Add ties as follows: Using assorted colours, with two strands held together, join with ss 10 sts from centre, passing hook beneath coat-hanger wire, ch20, fasten off and cut yarn leaving 20cm yarn tassle.

Add 2 ties at points 1 and 7 on diagram.

Attaching To The Bike

As bicycle handlebars and posts vary quite a bit depending on the type of bike, you may have to bend the hook to fit. My mountain bike has a handlebar extension and so the hook fitted really well around the handle bar post. Tie the bike basket on to the handlebars with the ties provided and stand back and admire!

Hints and Tips /Special Instructions

Before beginning the crochet, bend the coathanger into an approximate outline shape for the frame as follows; Form a bend halfway along each of the shoulder straight edges, then do the same with the bottom edge.

When shaping the base, don't forget at the beginning of each row, skip the stitch directly beneath the turning chain so the next stitch is the first stitch in the pattern and finish each row with a stitch into the turning chain of the previous row.

When working the sides, fasten off at the end of each round and weave in the ends, turn after each round so that you are alternately working on the inside and the outside of the basket.

Change colour every row and increase as directed every third row.

Stitch Marker Positions

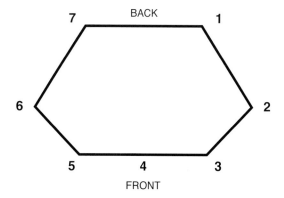

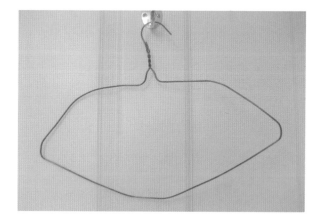

Peachy
by Ruby McGrath

Ruby says:

I love getting out on my bike in the sun, with my daughter attached to the back with her giant helmet on. I'm very proud of my pretty bike, so what better way to spruce her up than to make a little saddle cover and add a bit of personality.

The shades remind me of childhood peach lemonade, and it keeps my bottom nice and comfy, even on the longest of rides!

Yarn:

Rowan All Seasons Cotton

262 Burnt Orange   **261 Cosmos**   **182 Bleached**

(A) - Burnt Orange (262) x 1 ball
(B) - Cosmos (261) x 1 ball
(C) - Bleached (182) x 2 balls

Tension:

1 motif measures 9cm across

Materials:

4mm (UK 8/US 6)

Sizes:

Finished saddle cover will stretch to fit up to a 30cm wide, 38cm long seat.

Peachy Motifs (make 7)

Rnd 1: Using A, make a magic ring and work 12tr into it. Fasten off. (12 sts)

Rnd 2: Join B with ss anywhere around the circle, 1ch. Work 1 puff st into same sp then into each st around (12 puff sts). Join with ss into top of first puff st. Fasten off.

Rnd 3: Join C with ss into any 2ch sp, 3ch, work 3tr into same 2ch sp, work 4tr in next 2ch sp then in each 2ch sp around.

Weave in all ends and gently block to measurements.

Construction

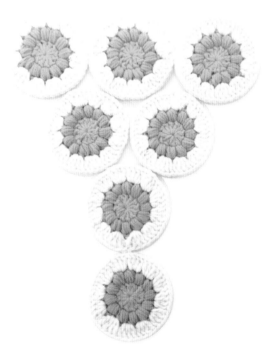

Lay the 7 circles out flat to form a triangle. Using a tapestry needle and yarn C, stitch circles together in sp between 4tr clusters of round 3. You will need to attach circles together in a total of 9 places.

Border

Set-up round: Lay your triangle flat, as seen. Using A, and working into sp between the two 4tr clusters at top of right hand corner circle, 12ch, ss into top of middle circle to the left in sp between the 4tr clusters, 12ch. Ss into the top of left hand corner circle, in sp between the 4tr clusters. Fasten off.

Ss into side of same circle in sp between the 4tr clusters, 12ch, ss into middle of left middle circle in sp between the 4tr clusters, 12ch, ss into side of bottom circle, in sp between the 4tr clusters. Fasten off and weave in ends.

Ss into opposite side of same circle in sp between 4tr clusters, 12ch, ss into side of middle right circle in sp between 4tr clusters, 12ch, ss into side of top right circle, ch3 and continue working in rounds as follows:

Rnd 1: 1tr in next and each st including chains to end, ss into top of tc. Fasten off.

Rnd 2: Join B with ss into any st around edge, 3ch, 1tr in each st around, ss into top of tc, 3ch.

Rnds 4 and 5 (optional depending in the size of your bike seat): Rep row 3.

You should work these rows until the cover hangs slightly over the depth of your bike seat.

Rnd 6: Pull the sides around the seat, and using B, match up 16 sts around the point of the seat, ss them together (see page 64). This creates a pocket that should fit snugly over the point of the seat, 3ch.

Rnd 7: Work tr2tog in each st around and rep this rnd if necessary to secure the cover around the bike seat then ss into top of tc. Fasten off.

Weave in the ends.

Special instructions

Puff Stitch: Work as 4htr, secured using a 2ch as follows: [Yarn over hook and pull up a loop] 4 times, yarn over and pull through all loops on hook, 2ch.

Verity says:

For me, a pair of handlebar streamers fluttering in the wind as a bike zooms by has be the ultimate in bike accessories.

Fun and great for the kids, these bright handlebar streamers are an easy one night project. The slipstitch colour pattern is great for beginners as you only use one colour in a row.

Yarn:

Rowan All Seasons Cotton

248 Strawberry   **246 Hedge**   **255 Summer**   **249 Denim**

(A) - 248 Strawberry
(B) - 246 Hedge
(C) - 255 Summer
(D) - 249 Denim

1x 50g ball of each colour

Tension:

16 sts = 10cm/ 4 inches measured over stocking stitch

Materials:

5mm circular 80cm long or DPNs (whichever is preferred for working small circumferences in the round)

Stitch marker

Sizes:

To fit around grip 11cm/ 4.5in in circumference snugly but this pattern is easily customizable (see Hints and Tips)

Leaving a 30cm/12in tail and using A and the Pinhole Cast On, cast on 9 sts. Join in the rnd and PM for beg of rnd.

Knit 1 rnd.

Next rnd: (Kfb) around. 18 sts

Work Rnds 1-6 of Slip Stitch Colour Pattern, breaking yarn at beginning and end of each rnd and leaving each tail at least 30cm/12in long.

Cont in Slip Stitch Colour Pattern (carrying yarn inside of work when not in use instead of breaking off), working Rnds 1-6 eight times more, or however many repeats necessary to fit your handlebar grip.

Change to A and knit 2 rnds. Cast off and weave in cast off end.

Pull remaining tails through the cast on hole and then pull the hole tight to close.

Repeat for other handlebar grip.

Slot on to the handlebars of your bike and be the envy of the neighbourhood!

Special instructions

Slip each slipped st p-wise.

Pinhole Cast On (also known as the Emily Ocker Circular Cast on)

You can use either a crochet hook or a knitting needle for this method. Thanks to Emily Wessel and Alexa Ludeman of Tin Can Knits, I now prefer the knitting needle method, which is the one I'll share with you here. For a more in-depth tutorial from Tin Can Knits go to **http://blog.tincanknits.com/2012/05/25/pinhole-cast-on-tutorial/**

First, make a circle using the end of your yarn. Pinch the circle in your LH, and hold the needle and working yarn in your RH. You will create new stitches using the point of the needle, working into the centre of the circle.

1. Insert needle into circle from front to back
2. Wrap yarn around needle
3. Use needle point to bring loop through circle from back to front (1 new loop on needle)
4. Wrap working yarn around needle point (2 loops on needle)
5. Use finger to lift first loop over second loop and off the needle : 1 loop remains, this is one stitch cast-on

Rep Steps 1-5 until the required number of stitches are on your needle. You might find it a bit fiddly at first, but it will soon fall in to place, and will have mastered a very useful circular cast on which prevents holes in the centre of your work.

Slip Stitch colour pattern

Rnd 1: With A, knit.

Rnd 2: With B, *k1, sl1 wyib; rep from * to end.

Rnd 3: With B, *p1, sl1 wyib; rep from * to end.

Rnd 4: With C, knit.

Rnd 5: With D, *sl1 wyib, k1; rep from * to end.

Rnd 6: With D, *sl1 wyib, p1; rep from * to end.

Rep these 6 rnds for patt.

Hints & tips

Use cast on tail as a guide to make measuring tails during first 6 rounds of colour pattern easier.

Customize the fit of your streamers by casting on half the number of stitches needed to fit around the circumference of your handlebar grip. You can also make them longer by doing more repeats of the slip stitch colour pattern.

Schematic

1x1 rib	k1, p1 ribbing		**p2tog**	Purl two together
2x2 rib	k2, p2 ribbing		**patt**	Pattern
alt	Alternate		**pm**	Place marker
approx	Approximately		**prev**	Previous
beg	Beginning		**psso**	Pass slipped stitch over
CC	Contrast colour		**pu**	Pick up
cdd	Centred double decrease - slip 2 stitches knitwise together, knit 1, pass slipped stitches over		**rem**	Remaining
			rep	Repeat
			Rev St st	Reverse stocking stitch
cm	Centimetres		**RH**	Right hand
CN	Cable needle		**rm**	Remove marker
C2B	Cable 2 backwards – sl st onto CN, hold in back, k1 from LH needle, k1 from CN		**rnd(s)**	Round(s)
			row	Row
C2F	Cable 2 forwards – sl st onto CN, hold in front, k1 from LH needle, k1 from CN All cable stitches to follow this format but to be included in special abbreviations for that pattern		**RS**	Right side
			sk	Skip
			sk2p	Slip 1, knit 2 together, pass slipped stitch over
			skp	Do not use – use ssk instead unless you have very good reason!
cont	Continue		**sl**	Slip stitch
dec('d)	Decrease(d)		**slm**	Slip marker
DPN	Double pointed needle		**ssk**	Slip one knitwise, slip one purlwise, knit two slipped stiches together
foll	Following			
g	Grammes		**ssp**	Slip one, slip one, purl two slipped stitches together
G st	Garter stitch			
in	Inches		**st**	Stitch
inc	Increase. Use only in descriptions e.g. "inc in this way on each row…" or "Row 8 (inc row)". For instructions, please specify which increase to use e.g. "K1, m1, k12…" or "K1, kfb, k12…"		**St st**	Stocking stitch
			tbl	Through back loop
			tog	Together
			w&t	(Wrap and turn). Bring yarn to the front between the needles, slip the next st purlwise, take yarn to back between the needles, turn work, slip st back from LH to RH needle.
incl	Including			
k	Knit			
k-wise	Knitwise		**WS**	Wrong side
kfb	Knit one through the front then through the back (same stitch)		**wyib**	With yarn in back
			wyif	With yarn in front
k2tog	Knit two together		**yb**	Take yarn to back of work
LH	Left hand		**yo**	Yarn over
m1	(Make one) Pick up strand between sts from the back and place on LH needle. Knit into this strand.			
mb	Make bobble			
MC	Main colour			
p	Purl			
p-wise	Purlwise			

knitting abbreviations

ch	Chain
blo	Back loop only
dc	Double crochet
dc2tog	Double crochet 2 stitches together (decrease 1 stitch)
flo	Front loop only
htr	Half treble crochet
rep	Repeat
RS	Right side of work
sc	Single crochet
sk	Skip
ss	Slip Stitch
sp	Space
st(s)	Stitch(es)
tr	Treble crochet
tr2tog	Treble crochet 2 stitches together (decrease 1 stitch)
tc	Turning chain
WS	Wrong side of work

crochet abbreviations

thank you

to...

Team Rayfield: Kate, Jono, Florrie and Bea. Not only are you wonderful friends, but you make beautiful models too!

Rowan Yarns for their fantastic support, supplying gorgeous yarns, giving us some great advice and getting on board with a(nother) crazy baa ram ewe idea.

Our designers, who have made this whole book possible, with an extra mention to the lovely Rachel Coopey who has always been on hand for advice. You're special. In a good way.

Our two fabulous tech editors Ashley Knowlton and Rachel Atkinson, casting their beady eyes over our patterns with the computer equivalent of a big red pen.

The 'props department'! Thanks to Katherine Johnnson, Adrian Taylor, Robberttown Community Centre Preschool, Ruby McGrath and The Rayfields for lending us their super cool bikes and bike bits.

Chris Britton, for managing to do the stunning layout for this book without causing irreconcilable differences with his wife. Just.

And all the staff and customers of baa ram ewe whose unwavering support fuels our creativity and allows us to do so many exciting woolly things!

V & J